10 Steps to Get Over Dick Head

Recover Your Courage, Confidence & Happiness!

Welcome Change. Find Your Purpose.
Heal with Humor.

Debbie Seagle

10 Steps to Get Over Dick Head © Copyright <<2023>> DOiT Publishing, LLC.

For more information on bulk buy discounts, contact deb@lifebackdoit.com
https://www.lifebackdoit.com.

ISBN: Paperback 978-1-958685-05-1

DISCLAIMER:

This is a self-help book. Help yourself to the ideas and concepts.

It is written from a woman's perspective, intended to amuse and provoke thought, reflection, and healing. Any advice given in this book is an offering from someone with healthy battle scars and is not professional in the sense that educated theories are presented in any way.

Inspiring joy and laughter however are my profession. So, you can take the enclosed self-deprecating disclosures as professionally tested solutions to finding a better way to live, improve, and enjoy your life.

This book may contain adult content including but not limited to instruction for violent behavior directed at your pillow, advanced laughing techniques that could lead to peeing one's pants, and linguistic descriptivism.

No abstract nouns were harmed in the making of this list of disclaimers. All research was conducted reliably, and usually safely and ethically.

Any user of anything I suggest assumes the full risk of insult, injury, embarrassment, and legal consequences resulting from performing any activity in this book. I will only be held accountable for my own actions. You do whatever makes you happy. Hopefully, everything you do from now on will make you happy!

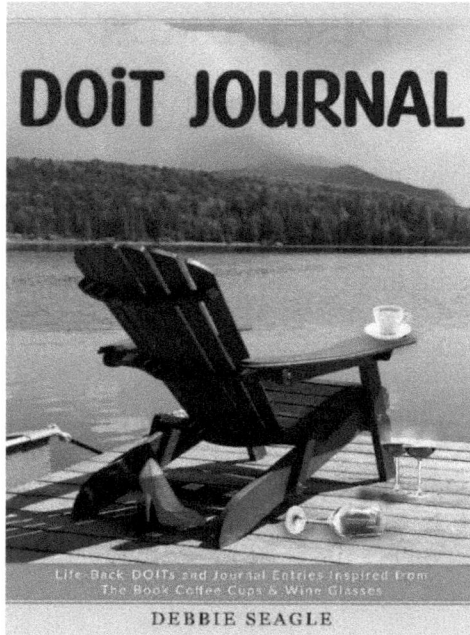

A Gift for You!

Get Your Free DOiT Journal at
www.lifebackdoit.com

Includes Journal Prompts & DOiTs inspired by the book
Coffee Cups & Wine Glasses

If you enjoy this book, I'd love to hear from you. When you reach the last page, please leave a review and follow me. I'm not sure where I'm going, but just Follow me; it won't be boring!

If you don't enjoy this book, heck, I didn't really write it. My dog's cousin did. She's an idiot.

Table Of Contents

INTRODUCTION

DOiT

A "DOIT" is an obsolete Dutch coin of little value. But when you DOiT, you will gain significant value. That's why I encourage you to DOiT throughout this Guide to Becoming You Again.

Aside: In the book, *Coffee Cups & Wine Glasses*, DOiTs are life hacks and fun activities.

DOiT Journal

Seriously, or jokingly, stop and indulge in the Journal prompts after each chapter. Take a pause to reconnect with yourself and rediscover who you are. Writing it down to look back on later will give you a boost in mindfulness, memory, and communication skills. You'll be surprised when you observe what you didn't know about yourself. DOiT.

It will also boost your IQ, help you learn from your past, plan for your future, relieve stress, and reduce belly fat. Oh, well, maybe not the belly fat. But you will benefit in other ways when you stop to reflect and write your responses in the DOiT Journal.

Here's your first DOiT Journal entry to get you started:

DOiT Journal:

- What was the best day of your life (so far)? You may not have lived it yet!

- Write down your 5 favorite things about yourself:

It could be courage, ability, determination, your unique talent to touch your toes or whistle through your nose?

- What is the most memorable compliment you have ever received?

What's Holding you Back?

Your heart was stomped on too? After that forever relationship ends, there's not much left to do but to find a new purpose for your life, drink wine, and dance naked in the rain (in Dick Head's front yard).

Well, it may not *be **that** much fun*. But if you use the following strategies, you will begin to make new decisions to live a magnificent life that takes you somewhere more advantageous than his front yard.

If you're reading this, you probably know it's over. Maybe you want it to be over.

You may not be able to admit it yet, because if you admit it, then what?

When 30 years of marriage evaporated, it changed my life, forever. Lord knows I was devastated and, well … simply not functioning (at first). Being ousted isn't easy. It is freaking traumatic and there is no clear path to recovery.

To contradict my confession that there's not a paved trail, I have outlined a simple road map for YOU to get over Dick Head. This recovery system is as limitless as the reality of driving your own life, going your way, facing the facts, finding strength, and making *your* decisions for your exciting destination. Go forward.

That's the best thing about your life now: it's all about you. Where will you go? What will you do?

It's your decision.

That's empowering!

Your inner magnificence will emerge again, so you can learn what *you* think and who *you* are. Decide what *you* want. I repeat (again); it's Your Decision.

"You only live once, but if you do it right, once is enough." ~ Mae West

Also, imagine while rediscovering your life that you have no friends, family, or pets to care for. Just oblige yourself and find some **alone time** to venture into accepting the dares I'm challenging you with – to start your new life … and get over Dick Head.

We. Women can endure the trauma of a broken heart, shattered wine glass, expanding butt, aging parents, menopause, thinning eyebrows, chin hair, and cellulite. That's just a Smither of what gives us unbelievable dynamism. Divorce should be a piece of cake (not an entire cake).

Like childbirth, just realize that no one can do it for you. It's your pain to deal with; you're on your own there. But countless women have done it and you can too! You're never alone. You never have been.

We're in this together, bound by the ridiculous bodily functions, accompanied by the emotional consequences, and doused with the unexpected crap dumped on us, especially now. Face it – it's a dang low point in our journey, but it will change. For the better.

Change moves you forward. Progress with purpose, rather than simply letting life knock you around into whomever you will become next. Take a spin, turn the corner, let it go, and start living with hope and happiness. Keep going, I'm with you.

When I was discarded like a dead plant obliviously basking in the sun, 10 Steps were my self-indulgent haphazard growth and recovery discovery to reckon with the dejection (yeah, it was that confusing and cumbersome). But self-indulgence isn't hopelessly selfish; it is a God-given right to women who've been shit upon.

I, at least, have the decency to transfer withered plants into the compost pile. Some are resilient enough to root in the manure and grow again.

Are you following the simile metaphor allusions here? When you're thrown into a pile of shit, it enriches your roots and allows you to blossom in an unlikely environment. It's your opportunity to rejuvenate your life. Discard the crap and get to blooming.

As you read, you will experience the phases of finding yourself again and discover that you have found your better self. In your fear, I hope you find your courage. I hope you find humor in what made you sad and something beautiful in the ugly parts of your life. Look for it; courage, humor, and beauty are all in you, waiting to be released.

Stick a badge of courage on your chest and find yourself again. You've got this. Use the following 10 steps to get your life back and get over Dick Head.

Step 1
Cry Baby

"Heaven knows we need never be ashamed of our tears, for they are rain upon the blinding dust of earth, overlying our hard hearts. I was better after I had cried, than before—more sorry, more aware of my own ingratitude, more gentle." ~ Charles Dickens

I read somewhere that the faint scent of a woman's tears can reduce sexual arousal in men. What the mother of stupidity are we supposed to do with that? Also, scientists say that animals can't cry. But crocodiles shed tears when they eat. Chew on that awhile. (I should have deleted this paragraph, but I thought you should know.)

After all that you've been through, allow yourself to cry. You may as well allow it. You're going to do it anyway. Human crying is a safe and effective way to wash away your tears. Find a private crying place and allow yourself to cry long, hard, and unashamedly.

Give yourself permission to let go. Give in. Hurt. Rip your guts out. Feel so miserably alive that you doubt your mortality. You can be dramatic. Scream with your cry if it helps.

The crying process is one of the most important steps to getting over Dick Head. It really works and involves very little effort. You can call it quits when you've had enough. Get it done and get it over with.

After the whammy, you are likely to cry effortlessly, unexpectedly, and hysterically off and on. But sooner or later, you do have to stop crying, baby! Truth is: you really can't decide when. You'll stop when you run out of tears.

And you will.

So, cry.

If it's not happening, try these non-scientific crying prompts to get started if (for some crazy reason) you haven't cried, or you're out of practice:

- Make sure you're not dehydrated (fill up your favorite wine glass).

- Designate a crying place.

- Make a crying face:

- Close your eyes and scrunch your face.

- Turn the corners of your lips down and force the inner corners of your eyebrows upwards.

DOiT.

If this doesn't make you laugh, you may be on your way to a good cry. If you have small children near you, at least you will make *them* cry. (That's why you need to find some time *alone,* in your private crying spot.)

Now, open your mouth widely, with the corners of your mouth pointing downward (like Lucille Ball), and make waaaaa crying noises. It may help to get an "I Love Lucy" episode and repeatedly play a scene where she is bawling. Turn up the volume. After ten minutes of this, you should be able to cry.

If the tears still don't flow, try cutting onions. Put them behind a fan. Put your face in front of it and make a weeping noise into the fan. Ok, that may make you laugh. Either way, you're making the proper noise. *Besides, who doesn't love wailing into a fan!*

Sit under a waterfall and cry for dramatic gushing. If you don't have a handy waterfall, spend a good 36 minutes in the shower with water running down your face … commit to the tears. Pull it from your soul.

It's not helpful to curse in the shower when you're trying to cry. Cursing relieves stress. So does crying. Choose one or the other, unless you're really good at multitasking.

If you're not weeping yet, you are hopeless. Insult yourself about your inability to cry. Cry about that!

I was hoping it wouldn't come to this, but as a last resort for non-criers, poke your eyeball or get someone to kick you in the shin. If you're still dry-eyed, crying may not be your thing. You may have to enlist someone to DOiT for you.

I hope you have found your crying place and let it all go by now. If so, once you've cried as much as you can, and you'd like to stop the incessant relentless weeping and self-pity, avoid your crying place – unless it has become the shower. Then heck, I don't know what to tell you. Take a bath with a glass of wine, and don't get back in the shower until your glass is empty. It's difficult to drink in the shower anyway.

DOiT Journal:

- When was the last time you cried?

- What made you cry?

- What were you thinking?

- Was it worth crying about?

- Why?

- Why Not? (This is a valid question – answer it)

Step 2
Mad Breath

"Breathe. Let go. And remind yourself that this very moment is the only one you know you have for sure." ~ Oprah Winfrey

Breathing is a universal commonality among humans. It's also habit-forming. But before you can breathe freely, you've gotta get mad. Being mad is good for depression and enhances your health; sometimes it's good exercise too.

Scream, swear, holler, clean out, throw and break things (but not anything you have the slightest attachment to; it's not yourself you want to punish). Don't ever break your coffee cups or wine glasses. That would be a different kind of mad.

Let go of the rage hiding behind your public smile. Stomp your feet. Vent (mostly to yourself, alone) then breathe…

Releasing hostility is good for you – if you don't kill anyone. People who experience adversity are much more captivating. Those who've endured heartbreak have more strength of mind than the person (we all know her) with the perfectly perfect life.

Escaping a bad relationship gives you a depth of character that many never achieve. It also gives you ulcers. But congratulate yourself that you are even more delightfully compelling and fascinating now because of the calamities you have survived. Thank all the people who gave you depth-by-distress, then wave them away.

Psychiatrists say that if you never get mad, you won't live as long. Well, screw that! So, take a deep breath and throw a hissy fit to add more years and satisfaction to your life. Swear like it's your birthright (especially if you use words that shock you, make you blush, and ultimately repair your spirit).

Shower cursing is appropriate here. Remember, do this alone so you don't scare anyone (or get committed to a mental hospital).

How to throw a good tantrum:

It helps if you're hormonal. Better results are achieved during PMS or in the throes of menopause. But you don't have to wait for your body to approve and assist. Betrayed women can muster up a good conniption fit without mother nature. That is the beauty of being a woman.

1. As with crying, the first step is to make a face. This time it's not a sad face, it's a mad face. So, take a deep breath and pull your lips into a thin grimace over your gums and show your bottom teeth.

2. Squint your eyes and tighten the space between your eyebrows.

3. Roar and growl while visualizing Dick Head and/or Her.

4. Yell. Some great mantras to shout include: "You scum-sucking baboon-breath jerk-face cheating Dick Head!" Or my personal favorite: "I hope your dick falls off in front of a crowd!"

5. Punch a pillow. Draw his face on it and take it outside. Roll around in the mud with it. Stomp it... laugh at it... insult it with the glorified confidence of a banshee.

That should do it.

Just don't go all-out irrational and break someone's face. Promise yourself that. Think of your mad-ass rage as *Assertive Diva Ninja* orientation – and keep control. Then, after recovering from your conniption fit, you ARE in control. What a feeling!

If getting mad doesn't work for you, then revert to the tried and true ... don't get mad, get even. The best way to get even is to completely forget about Dick Head and start making your own world a party full of happiness. What a wonderful place to be! Especially since Dick Head isn't invited.

Take a breath. Don't think about what Dick Head is doing or with whom he is doing it (anymore). Just don't. Most importantly, don't drag your children and loved ones into it. Do not let them be sad with you. Trust me, you'll thank yourself later for having the strength to spare them.

Your goal is to stop breathing out of a paper bag.

After all the madness, you can finally breathe more easily.

Breathe for two minutes.

Well…maybe you should breathe longer. Yeah, keep breathing from now on. But….

1. Breathe in peace and serenity.

2. Breathe out hostility and madness.

3. Breathe in for 4 counts through your nose (peace, serenity)

4. Hold your breath for 4 counts (you have control and confidence)

5. Slowly release your breath through your mouth for 6 counts (release hostility and frustration)

6. Repeat

Breathe until you get bored – or pass out.

Passing out always relaxes you.

You should be feeling a lot better now. Beware the blaring signs that you're still not okay though, like if you forgot to shave the other leg while you were crying in the shower. Then again, you could have been too busy cursing to even bother shaving that leg that no one sees anymore. Who gives a whoop-ass if your legs are shaven anyway.

If you run around the neighborhood in your PJs cursing and crying hysterically, you've gone too far with the getting mad/crying exercises. You need to immediately skip to Step 8 and LOL.

If you laugh and rant out loud when you're home alone, it's an indication that you're finding your humor again. Or maybe you're just drunk. Hopefully, you're getting past the mad stage. You're not crazy; you're just entertainingly wacky. You know you're hilarious. Now you're okay.

Breathe.

Breathing helps you live longer.

Now, skip through the backyard, then pour yourself a glass of wine. I dunno, maybe you should have done that first?

DOiT Journal

- What makes you happy (that you're still breathing)?

- List all the reasons you can breathe freely now that Dick Head is history.

- Name some things that you won't allow to upset you again.

Step 3
A Little Help from Your Friends

"A friend is someone who doesn't speak in long complicated sentences, instead, she gets right to the point with phrases like "Poop on Dick Head; let's drink wine." ~ Debbie Seagle

You'll get by with a little help from your friends. One of the priceless riches in life is a true friend. Studies have shown that chimpanzees, baboons, horses, elephants, and dolphins make friends for life. In fact, whales literally have BFFs (best friends forever)!

When your relationship is over, your BFFs will give you advice, but you don't necessarily need to take it. They are sometimes out for revenge (on your behalf). They want to help you, and it's easy for them to come up with ideas for spiteful counterattacks. They don't have to DOiT.

Just listen, then step back and go with your true nature. If you're not the bitch they want you to be, so be it. You know in your heart what you would do if you were thinking clearly at this point. You are, or soon will be, a rational mending goddess.

Breakup or divorce can strip you of not only your secure family life and your dignity, but it spins up your social circle too. You will quickly recognize your true friends. They're the ones who tell you how stupid and dowdy Dick Head's slut is.

Couples may not invite you to dinner parties anymore. You're a threat now because you're an extraordinary single woman who may be lonely. Don't waste your energy trying to win anyone over.

Create your own alliances. Beautiful. You can pick and choose who you want to spend time with from now on.

Your mission is to stop striving to please everyone. You know that's what you were – the pleaser. But you don't have to be that self-sacrificing gratifier anymore! Dick Head has a new doormat. Let him walk all over *her* at the parties. Your true friends will act out how she embarrassed him by calling him *Snookie-do* in front of your "friends."

Just be you (the loving, happy, hopeful you). Only you really know what to do about your situation, and you are the person who will live with the decisions you make. So, take others' advice with a sip of wine (in a magnificent wine glass).

Then try to think about something else for a few hours. To hang on to your sanity, you must eventually stop making every conversation about your plight. Don't drive your girlfriends crazy enough to move to a secluded island and block your number. Let them speak, occasionally, about something other than your broken heart or your hidden desire to kick him in the nuts.

If you're still being offered guidance after you've had your fill, only take advice from people you would trade places with. Think about that.

I'd trade places with Matthew McConaughey's wife. But she never answered my letters, (and tweets, Facebook posts, postcards, and radio announcements) requesting to trade places with her.

I'll share Matthew's advice anyway: to "just keep livin'." Alright. Alright. Alright.

Stop talking and just keep livin' by reconnecting and getting involved in something new and fun… like photography, skydiving, quilting, or balloon animal-making (there must be groups for that). Join a book club, a ski club, or the Red Hat Society. Learn Tai Chi or play an instrument. Create something. If you make new friends, you don't need to even mention Dick Head. That gives you the freedom to practice leaving him behind.

The best part about just livin' is that you get to make your own decisions now. Don't give up that power! Your life: your decisions to make about it. Don't immediately latch on to a romantic relationship to fill your void. You have wine for that.

Remember those ideas you had when you were 6, 16, and 26? You had dreams for the life you would live. You probably scrapped most of your ambitions to please and appease someone. (Dick Head?)

If you get involved with someone before you recover the strength and willpower you had as a young woman, it will be hard to truly find it again. Focus on your own ideas and be your own person first. Become *You* again.

Stand on your own two stilettos and fill your pretty little head with plans for what you will do. Plan your own escapades and pursue adventures that excite *you*. Your future.

Know that you will be whatever you want to be now. Don't let anyone take your wiggle or your skip away from you again. Keep it and use it to be yourself and do anything you ever imagined you could.

Take this new life of yours and renew your neglected friendships. Visit with your friends or find a new one, and ultimately learn to live with yourself. Encourage your friends as well as yourself and support your own thoughts and dreams. You are majestic.

Become your own best friend, and there's no doubt you'll always be there for yourself! Like, where would you go anyway?

Now, begin building your own group of friends without Dick Head. Photocopy your smashed happy face and give it to someone at work, or a random passer-by. You could make a new friend! Or you could just strike up a conversation with someone new who thinks you're a weirdo.

DOiT Journal:

- Who are your best friends?

- How do you describe a True friend?

- How do you think your friends would describe you?

(Ask your friends how they think of you as a friend and use their answers to become a better friend.) It also validates how awesome you thought you were. And You Are.

Step 4
Honestly. Let it Go

"It's hard to fall into the habit of being honest with yourself when it's less painful to pick yourself up and run away like nothing really happened."
~ Debbie Seagle

Be honest. Once you face the truth, you let the deception go. Be honest with your friends, therapist, proctologist, and family about what you're going through. Honesty puts facts and feelings in perspective (but, again, not so many times that people start jumping into traffic when they see you coming). Now be truthful with yourself.

Just maybe, you *possibly* could have had a little bit of something to do with a reason the relationship died, fizzled, or blew up. It started out with elation and excitement. Then you grew closer and happier. Then something happened – or didn't happen.

Do you suppose going through this is so hard because you didn't honestly forgive, completely, when you said you would? Those resentments dangled in the background. You didn't forget either. Maybe that grudge made you cynical and suspicious. Maybe he was a Dick Head.

Use glue stick instead of lipstick on your lips occasionally. Listening in silence could say more than your clever comebacks. The words ``silent" and "listen" have the same letters.

But then again, maybe he just stopped communicating. Maybe you did too. Crickets.

Maybe you could have been a little more understanding, light-hearted, firm, fair, funny... Maybe you were, and everything still went wrong! If so, be less critical of yourself. Who are YOU to judge (yourself). It doesn't really matter – because you are moving forward with your own objectives now.

Spend less time making excuses for why he betrayed you. You probably should have ended it a lot sooner and stopped pretending that there was a way to salvage the dying dragon (you know there had to be a dragon in your story somewhere).

Whatever you did right or wrong, make it easier on yourself and forget. Forgive yourself. Even forgive the trashy tramp who stole your future, your husband, and your retirement plan. Forgive him for stripping you of your family, lifestyle, security, and sanity.

Forgiving doesn't mean "it's ok." It means you release it. It's nothing you will think about again. Let's change the word forgiveness to "f*ck it; I'm over it." That's more realistic.

Let it go.

Stop fantasizing about her breast implants rupturing at a cocktail party. Stop thinking about her altogether. Start thinking about what *you* will do now. Have confidence in *yourself.*

Stop thinking about Dick Head falling on his face into a septic tank. That's not going to make things better – or worse. It will, however, create entertaining visual images to fall back on.

Nothing can change. It's already your past. It has passed.

Disengage when he insults or belittles you. Never raise your voice (especially if he's yelling at you). That will confuse the hell out of him.

If you don't get the last word, that leaves him with the last hurtful remark, which never feels good. But it also leaves him the next card to play ... the apology card. Leaving the next move to him is a powerful strategy, even if he never shows his cards. It's a gamble, and you win by not playing his game. Shed your poker face, smile, and walk away.

Stop thinking you lost him. Honestly, He let You get away. (My) statistics confirm: he will discover what a magnificent, thrilling, loving, amazing person he let go of (you).

He will likely realize how much he needed you when he's clueless about things like what to get his mom for her birthday ... when she was born ... or her mailing address.

Just when you think you're out – you get pulled back in. It happens. He starts being nice to you. He didn't really mean that you dress like your grandmother. He says calling you hippo-butt was just playful teasing. You think: *We all screw up; shouldn't I give him another chance, again?*

The number of times you're willing to forgive is up to you.

We always hold on to hope, don't we? There is a possibility that you can make it work. But if you've given all the chances you had to give, made a fool of yourself, and his gallivanting was apparent to everyone but you: it's time to admit it's over. This step may seem out of place, and some find it more helpful in the very beginning, but optimism pushed this step way back here for me.

I gave Dick Head nine chances too many. But I was just blindly following my heart. He was cheating, but it was Her fault. He demeaned my thoughts and actions, but maybe he was right? Everything he didn't like about himself was my fault. *Of course, it was.*

He erased my confidence. I wasn't thinking. Follow your heart but use your brain a little more than I did. That may help you get your life back sooner. Have confidence in your own intuitions.

A Dick Head will try to make you feel bad when they're feeling guilty. I refused to believe that the guy my friends never liked, the one I gave up my own aspirations for ... was bailing on me and our family in front of the world.

That wasn't supposed to happen. I thought maybe if I tried to fix it (again) I could save face? That's just ridiculous. *My face was fine.*

But when you're honest with yourself, it's easier to recognize when it's over. That is difficult. That's not fun. Just DOiT. It's the only way to get over Dick Head.

Think about it, reasonably. It doesn't matter what he says. What do you see and know? Don't let yourself get lost in that alternative universe where someone conjures up ridiculous fictitious crap.

They confidently declare it and may honestly believe that if they promote it enough, it becomes true. Puh-leeze. Leave that crap to the politicians.

Quite often, someone will accuse you of what they are guilty of. It's called projecting. We don't have enough ink to get into that bamboozlement.

You are a strong, decisive, sensational, sensible woman. Believe in truth, affirm reality, and make your own decisions, no matter what you have always done. Make a conscious change if doing what you've always done isn't what is best for you.

Gain strength in realizing that you no longer recognize or claim those uncertainties that made you feel so vulnerable. Unchain your power to control your thoughts, feelings, and future.

Then, face the Music. A Billy Joel song says that honesty is a lonely word. It can be, at first. Some things are just not easy to believe. But once you find sincerity and accept reality, you become free.

In contrast, saying it and, believing in something you strive for is confirmation that you can absolutely accomplish it. It's still not true until you actually DO IT though. DOiT.

Don't allow what you *wish* to be true – to trap you in a damaging, dishonest past. That's true for both politics and relationships. Take care of yourself. Acknowledge your progress. Celebrate it. Own it. Wiggle out a little interpretive dance.

The truth is that if you don't let go and realize that the situation is over, you won't move ahead. Allow yourself to forgive the idiots, bastards, and trash tramps. More importantly, forgive yourself for everything you regret. Honestly, we all know it was Dick Head's fault anyway.

DOiT Journal:

- What surprises you most about your life now?

- What in this world turned out the way you expected it would?

- What fact do you find hard to accept?

- How will you accept it now? (Since you know it's a fact!)

- What have you done to get your life back? If nothing, what will you do today?

Step 5
Go Solo Not Wacko

"See how nature – trees, flowers, grass – grows in silence; see the stars, the moon and the sun, how they move in silence...We need silence to be able to touch souls." ~ Mother Teresa

Become okay with being alone. So many people don't know how to do that. Peace and solitude give you the opportunity to reflect, alter the laws of the universe, and fart without embarrassment.

When you learn to be alone, you learn how to be transparent with yourself. You could learn to like yourself! Remember who you are. It's not like you're going to disapprove of your true self, are you? Hint: the answer is hell no.

Don't communicate in any way with anyone for an entire day, or more, if you can. This is crucial. Stop telling your friends about your breakup (they know about it now). You've committed to being honest with yourself, so tell the truth – that you are magnificent, and you are taking control of your life.

While you're spending time in your head, acknowledge what you've been thinking and let go of all feelings of loneliness, betrayal, desperation, fear, bitterness, shame, hopelessness, and all the other emotions that drag you down. You can't hide them; they will find you, so just go ahead ... claim them. If you own them, then they are yours to dispose of, right? DOiT.

Do you think you might have a few new feelings sliding in? I hope you feel courage, hope, freedom, clarity, pride, resolution, love, moxie, generosity, confidence, cheer, trust, joy, and relief.

You may as well admit it, while you have this time with yourself, that you are fabulous, genuine, delightful, thoughtful, worthy, beautiful, skillful, creative, hopeful, adorable, brilliant, charming, fun, kind, self-reliant, and are finding your sense of adventure again. Make these admissions your new perspective and add them to your DOiT Journal.

Perspective comes when you're not in the middle of a situation. That's why you are taking time to reposition and be alone. The best view of the Eiffel tower is not from the tower's observation deck. Observe your life from a higher angle.

There is always more than one way to look at every situation. Step back and look at how you're progressing, how you're feeling. Then work your way to the top to look down at what you left below. Wave goodbye and be where you are now.

Stand in front of a mirror and start telling yourself how stunning you are. Wink at yourself in the mirror and affirm yourself with well-deserved pick-up lines like:

- Hey baby, looks like you dropped something, my jaw
- If you were a triangle, you'd be "acute" one
- Guess what I'm wearing? The smile you gave me
- Are you a parking ticket? Because you've got FINE written all over you
- You are so sweet you could put Hershey's out of business
- I must be in heaven because I'm looking at an angel!

Believe it. Believe in yourself from now on. Practice accepting praise with gratitude, poise, and appreciation.

If you happen to unexpectedly fall into a relationship, make sure you have learned enough about yourself that you can introduce the true you. Be electrified by the way he makes you feel. Enjoy that sense of wonder and the excitement of being around him. If it's not there, well … you decide what you want to settle for. Let him be (just) your friend if he doesn't make your blood race. Think about it.

You need some time alone to appreciate who you are and feel it from deep within your heart. Get busy now and do a few more things by yourself. Clean out your sock drawer, smear an avocado all over your face, swim in the ocean, read a new book, get a massage, Get Over Dick Head, and Get Your Life Back. DOiT.

DOiT Journal:

Your feelings – they are a product of what you're thinking. Your feelings determine how you act and who you are. You know who you are; you are an independent, confident, majestic unicorn!

- OK, Ms. Awesome Pants, now You define yourself; who are you?

- What is the most fabulous thing about being alone with you?

- What words are all about You? Hint: I told you above.

Step 6
A Change Would Do You Good

"Change is inevitable. Growth is optional." ~ John Maxwell

Things change. That means that at any given moment, you are one decision away from a completely different life. You make your own decisions now. Be bold and make decisions that make your life splendid.

Space, freedom, and an unusually exciting or daring future ... that's what you can choose now. If it's what you want. Everything is possible, and nothing can hold you back. Well, your decisions can. Did you know that you can change your future by merely changing your attitude?

Most of the time, we fear change. Even change for the better. Sometimes we're afraid of letting ourselves (or someone else) down because we're living the life that's expected of us. It's comfortable. It's familiar and easier than ... what if?

So, we do nothing. And nothing changes. And the cycle of "what if?" continues.

Get outta town. Drive, just drive. Do it alone, if you dare. Or get your goofiest friend to go someplace with you. Take someone you don't have to cater to, and someone who doesn't take care of you either. Ride in a convertible like Thelma & Louise (just not over the cliff). Experience things you haven't – until now.

Escape. Just step outside. Sometimes a change in mindset is simply a change in scenery. Go antiquing; go hiking; go to a local theater production. Put some pink streaks in your hair.

Change your wine preference, your eye shadow, your underwear. Sit in the backyard. Book a weekend at a wellness spa (you've earned it). Camp outside under the stars.

Change makes life longer. It makes you more interesting. It makes you look at things differently. So, get over Dick Head already and make a change.

If you haven't made a plan for your new life yet, just get your ass in gear and do something. Anything! Put a smile on your face and get up this minute and move, dance, walk, run, twirl. Duhh, winning!

Begin by Forcing Yourself to:

- Get out of bed, off the couch
- Get out of your head
- Get out of your funk
- Get into your groove
- Get your favorite coffee cup; fill it up
- Get your favorite wine glass; Fill it to the middle of the widest width of the glass (that's the proper fill for a wine glass)
- Fake it 'till you make it
- Read and learn something new every day
- At least once a week, wear an outfit that makes you feel special. Wear your most fabulous clothes, underwear, and shoes. Do your hair, darken your eyebrows, put on makeup, and head out looking good. You'll be amazed at how different you feel and how your interaction with other people improves. It's because you have confidence and feel as if you're worth the effort.
- Physically de-clutter your life Take a weekend to clean your home as you never have before – ruthlessly ridding it of everything you no longer use. Get rid of his crap. Organize your house and put things where You want them to be. That's mentally refreshing! When your physical environment is in order, it's easier to unclutter your mind and get over Dick Head.
- Play the harmonica
- Create a story. If you have children, tell it to them

- Peel a banana with your feet
- Sculpt something with clay
- Cook something delicious from a book of old recipes
- Learn to do one thing well enough that you make it look easy It may take you a year, but it will be time well spent.

If you want to be good at something, figure out the best time to start. Don't waste your time figuring it out – the time is Now.

If something you once enjoyed doesn't really thrill you anymore, stop doing it.

It's time to discover your unfound talents and joys. It could be bowling, mini-golf, playing the tuba, kayaking, learning to sail, throwing a barbecue, or picnicking in a tree. The most important thing is that it's something that changes your normal routine and broadens your horizons.

Look online, in the newspaper, the DOiT Blog , or in a local magazine for ideas.

When life grabs you by the boobs and says, "come on, jump in," strip off your bikini and DOiT – move it, and move on.

If you work sitting in an office, get up every 58 minutes and stretch. Walk down the hall to peek at someone interesting. Get a drink of water.

It's not very exciting, but water really is a beneficial beverage, and tastes much better when you drink it from your wine glass. Water is great for hangovers, hydrates your skin, lubricates your joints, and is one of the cheapest ways to stay healthy. So put some H_2O in your wine glass a few times a day. Drink half of your body weight in ounces per day. I'm not being bossy; I'm just sharing what experts say you should drink. Good luck with that.

Changes you make will affect the people around you. Think about it. You could empower and make life better for everyone you care for by inspiring a new outlook and doing the unexpected.

Sometimes you want to (or need to) wallow in your misery. Ok, give yourself a day of leniency to eat garbage in front of the TV. Accomplish nothing. Sleep off-and-on all day. Don't clean the kitchen. A day. Not a week. It could ignite a recharge in you.

Sometimes you want action. Always, you need to change it up. Do whatever feels right, just be sure to move forward in a way you never have before. You are so worth it, and the change will do you good.

DOiT Journal:

- What is something new you've tried that you'll never regret?

- What 3 Changes will you make in your life this week?

- If you could change one thing about your daily routine, what would it be? DOiT! Then change another unfulfilling pattern next week

Step 7
You ARE The Greatest

"Never underestimate the power of dreams and the influence of the human spirit. We are all the same in this notion: The potential for greatness lives within each of us." ~ Wilma Rudolph

One morning you will awaken (that's a good move!) and you will feel good for no reason. Every day isn't going to be about your broken relationship. As they pass, your days will progressively become about the people you love, and about what you think. Want. Like.

If you want a little feel-good inspiration in three minutes, watch the Kenny Rogers music video "The Greatest" about the little boy who, day after day, believes he is going to succeed. He tosses the ball into the air, swings, and misses every dang time.

That little boy never loses hope, and he never gives up. He has no one to pitch to him; no one helps him. Yet he believes that he will succeed.

His mom calls him in for dinner and the little feller imagines that everything depends on his last bat. The world stands still as he throws the ball up and swings with all his might. He misses. Again.

But his takeaway? He missed hitting the ball because he's such an incredible pitcher!

That level of optimism and undying belief is what we were born with. As a child, we saw every possibility as a reality we could capture. Everything was remarkable, magical, and undoubtedly achievable.

Remember when the moon followed us around? Snuggling under a blanket protected us from monsters and anything else we were trying to escape. (That one, I still have reason to believe.)

Over your lifetime, you may have allowed failure and rejection to weigh down your confidence and ambition, but you can recover it again. Sometimes our unanswered prayers turn out to be what we actually need – even if we don't want it.

When an outcome isn't what you expect, look at it as if you were a child, and discover why it is ultimately better than what you thought you wanted. It's a wonderful game to play.

I spent my childhood dreaming that Davy Jones was singing his songs to *me* (hey hey, he was a Monkee). My dream came true when I spent an afternoon with Davy and his horse at Colonial Downs Race Track. That night, he dedicated a song and sang directly to me. I stood in front of the stage, gazing up at him, my arms dangling, and cried like a teenage girl (when I was 34).

I'm not sure if I was crying because my dream came true, or because he was two heads shorter than me. He was a terrible dancer, and he was an old man! That day was bitter-sweet. But I actually breathed the same air, he hugged me, and I talked to Davy Jones, in person!

It was exhilarating to be that excited child living my most extraordinary fantasy. I allowed myself to momentarily fall back into my young dream world where I was with Davy Jones.

Then my mom found me, handed me my baby, and I changed his diaper. She had a talent for jerking me back to reality. But I can still pull those dreamy feelings out whenever I want.

Hold on to thrilling moments as long as you can. Some dreams do come true, but they're not always what you imagined. Living a distorted dream teaches you to appreciate what you get. Allow yourself to enjoy it for what it is.

You may have grown up, but you can still decide what to grow into. Decide that you are the greatest by thinking greatly. When you are optimistic, you attract unexpected opportunities.

Interesting, uplifting people will want to be around you when your "feel good" energy naturally attracts more positive energy. It's a wonderful circle to get caught in. When people who drag you down come around, either lift them up or run away. Stay on a high level of hope and optimism, even if you do it by yourself at first.

There's nothing better than childish confidence and enthusiasm. If you can't easily capture it again by believing it's there, listen to some perky music. Music is like a push-up bra that lifts you up with absolutely no effort.

Create a playlist of inspiring tunes to brighten your attitude.

Make several lists of songs depending on your mood (joyful, rebellious, wild-woman, or chillin' – however you're feelin').

Here are Some of My Favorite Nostalgic, Sappy, Happy Tunes:

Joy To The World – Three Dog Night

I Get Knocked Down – Chumbawamba

What A Wonderful World – Louis Armstrong

I'm Into Something Good – Herman's Hermits

Amazing Grace – traditional

What A Feeling (Flashdance) – Irene Cara

Walking on Sunshine – Katrina and the Waves

Don't Worry, Be Happy- Bobby McFerrin

I'm A Believer – The Monkees

I Will Survive – Gloria Gaynor

Footloose – Kenny Loggins

A Beautiful Morning – The Rascals

Peaceful Easy Feeling – Eagles

I'm So Excited – The Pointer Sisters

Oh! What A Beautiful Morning! – From *Oklahoma!*

I've Got the World on A String – Frank Sinatra

The Greatest – Kenny Rogers

Girls Just Want to Have Fun – Cyndi Lauper

Do Wah Diddy – Manfred Mann

Blame It on Your Heart – Patty Loveless

Give a Little Bit – Supertramp

Getting Jiggy with It – Will Smith

I hope you are finding that optimistic joy of childhood again. You can you know. Believe that you are, because you are, The Greatest!

DOiT_Journal:

- Make Your playlist.

- What do you consider to be the Greatest thing you've ever done?

- What didn't go as you wanted it to, but turned out to be even better?

- What will you do next (something GREAT like – learn to juggle or design a comfortable bra that is actually comfortable)?

Step 8
LOL

"A smile starts on the lips, a grin spreads to the eyes, a chuckle comes from the belly; but a good laugh bursts forth from the soul, overflows, and bubbles all around." ~ Carolyn Birmingham

Did you know that people actually pay to laugh? It's called Laughing Yoga. Try it. Here's how it's done:

- Clapping while chanting "ho ho ha ha ha" then throwing your arms into the air and clapping to "very good… very good… yeaaah!"

- Breathe in while lifting your arms… laughing as you lower them

- Greeting laughter – Greet (wave and laugh) at someone – or do it in the mirror with yourself

- Argument laughter – Shake a finger at someone while laughing. (That is so confusing to me)

- Ants in your pants – That's my favorite … Imagine it, and do it while laughing

- Another yoga laughter exercise is both stupid and somewhat insightful: Time to laugh … look at your watch and laugh. Do that a few times each day. The stupidity of it may become funny to you.

  Inside scoop: As I edited this, I found "Time to Laugh" again (for about the 30teenth time, and it really *did* make me laugh!) Not everything happens instantly. Look at your wrist and laugh.

The rest of the warm-up exercises include childlike playfulness and laughing like a small child. Children laugh with their entire bodies. (That's pretty funny). This teaches you that there is always time to laugh.

If you're finding it difficult to laugh right now, I feel obligated to coach you into a laugh. I've already guided you through crying, getting mad, breathing, facing the facts, being with yourself, and letting go. I've encouraged you to change it up by peeling a banana with your feet. I feel like you may still need me if you haven't really laughed yet. It's Time to Laugh. DOiT.

Okay, start by raising your eyebrows (and widen your eyes). Sometimes this could kickstart a bout of laughter. It pretty much forces you to smile.

No?

Then…

SMILE.

Just stop right now, and slap a big stupid smile on your face, raising your eyebrows.

You may have to force it. But do it. SMILE! (Did you notice how your eyes open wide?)

Fake a laugh … Laugh now. Smile, and make laughing sounds. DOiT! Smile big & silly.

Now, Laugh.

Get in front of a mirror.

- Smile really big and look at the twinkle in your eyes.
- Smile bigger, get closer, wave at yourself, and laugh again.
- I'll bet you never noticed how your eyes sparkle when you laugh.

Go ahead, fake laugh for three minutes. It's good for you. Did you know your body doesn't recognize the difference between a fake and a real smile or laugh, thus the benefits are the same.

Laughing strengthens your immune system, your heart, and your attitude. It relieves stress, burns calories, and (possibly?) eliminates unwanted facial hair. Laughter inspires hope and helps you release anger, enabling you to forgive sooner and get over a Dick Head.

There are different types of laughter: So many, it's not funny.

Try these types of Laughter… Sound them out:

- Burst of Laughter
- Inappropriate Laughter
- Sarcastic Laugh
- Belly Laugh
- Awkward Laughter
- Nervous Laughter
- Snort
- Guffaw
- Snicker
- Chuckle
- Cackle
- Giggle
- And my personal favorite, the Baby Laugh…

Verbalize the above list one more time. Out Loud. DOiT.

You will feel better and have a residual smile to wipe off your face. Don't wipe it off!

Keep Going!

Get up now:

- Smile at yourself in the mirror again.
- Smile until you smile back at yourself.
- Laugh and stick your thumbs in your ears.
- Laugh at yourself, looking deeply into your eyes.

Laugh every day from now on! Even if you fake it. Just so you know, the thumbs in the ears laugh always makes me start laughing (especially when I stick my tongue out too).

I'm doing it every morning and will be laughing just knowing you are enjoying the same silly performance with me. I told you we were in this together!

When you find your funny, even in a fleeting moment, grab it and hold tight. Don't let it go until you can't stop laughing. And smiling. And rejoicing. That's some good ole Getting Over Dick Head right there.

Just be aware that laughter can be contagious. You want proof? Get with (or call) a friend and simply start laughing … don't say anything.

Keep laughing until they start, and it will be hard to stop! It must be with someone who gets you. Otherwise, they may refer you to a counselor (with no sense of humor).

I call and laugh with my best girlfriend who immediately laughs back for no reason. I also call my son. We started this laugh-at-nothing disorder when he was in high school. He may be considering having me put away now though. Maybe I do it too often?

Very few other actions lower your blood pressure, heal fungus (possibly) and medicate your pain like laughter does. That's why laughter is the best medicine (unless you have diarrhea).

When you finally forgive, you learn to smile again.

When you smile about the life you live, you end up living a life worth smiling about.

When you smile, it sometimes leads to laughter.

When you laugh and move on, you get over a Dick Head.

DOiT.

DOiT Journal:

- What makes you smile?

- What makes you laugh?

- Remember something outrageously funny (write it down).

- Think of something funny to do with or to someone (something you'll both laugh at).

Some ideas:

~ Next time you're in a public restroom, guard the paper towel dispenser in the name of a New Green Deal then offer to blow-dry people's hands with your mouth to save energy.

~ In your favorite department store, hide in the racks of clothing and grab people's ankles as they walk by.

Some ideas:

- Next time you're in a public restroom, guard the paper towel dispenser in the name of a New Green Deal then offer to blow-dry people's hands with your mouth to save energy.

- In your favorite department store, hide in the racks of clothing and grab people's ankles as they walk by.

You know just the thought of doing it is funny. DOiT. (First, refer to the disclaimer at the front of the book.)

Step 9
The Secret to Happiness

"Most people are about as happy as they make up their minds to be."
~ Abraham Lincoln

I read that quote when I was young. I believed it because it's true. I decided to simply be happy for the rest of my life. It's a thing. You can make that choice.

Now that you're not crying all the time, you can breathe. You've forgiven, laughed, and moved on. Your achievements have earned you the opportunity to learn the secret of genuine happiness.

It's the most fulfilling and simple activity in this book. Nothing you have done for yourself thus far comes close to filling your soul with as much joy. It's so obviously uncomplicated that you're not going to believe you've discovered anything new.

Maybe you haven't given it enough attention. Yet. You may not have considered the power of your ability to create a better world.

The secret to happiness is commonly known as an act of human kindness.

You may already know this. But true happiness is found in helping others … in making someone else happy. Giving to someone else will give you complete satisfaction. You are the secret to your own happiness – by doing something for someone else rather than focusing on yourself.

It's not how much you give, but how sincere you feel about the giving. When it comes from the heart, you will feel it, and so will the receiver.

Have you ever done something simple for someone without realizing how much it would mean to them? When you see the unspoken gratitude in their eyes and sense their appreciation for something that was really nothing … you feel genuine connection and warmth. It's an unintentional gift to yourself.

That must be what Mahatma Gandhi meant when he said, *"To find yourself, lose yourself in the service of others."*

Gifting sometimes seems a little selfish to me because it makes *me* happy. Conversely, I've always found it difficult to accept help, compliments, or gifts from other people – until someone said to me, "Don't deny me the joy of doing this for you." It stopped my breath. That was sincerity.

If you start feeling unfulfilled or sorry for yourself again, try making someone happy, or surprised, and see where it takes you. Turn your focus from yourself to someone else. Your life improves when you improve the life of another person. Nothing feels better. It's crazy how that happens, but it does.

My neighbor felt good about helping me quickly cut a tree with his chainsaw after watching me with my hand saw for an hour. He had a girlfriend over, and I was becoming a spectacle. I think it made him feel good to help me, and it got me out of the way at the same time! See how it works both ways?

Think about it: everyone is going through something. More than half the people you encounter have something worse happening in their life than what you're struggling with. It's hard to believe that anyone could feel more dejected and trampled than you have. Believe it. Realizing that someone may be grieving or suffering makes it easier to be kind to them.

Everyone is living through drama in one way or another. Recognize that and have empathy. But if they're just an asshole jerk and you can't resist the urge to flip them off, do it underneath your shirt or steering wheel.

There are so many little things you can do to brighten someone's day. Use some, or all of the following, simple ideas that lead to mutual happiness:

- Chase someone's runaway grocery cart (and give it back to them)

- Say something nice to the checkout clerk. That's always an easy one

- Mow your neighbor's side of the yard (if you know for sure that they hate mowing as much as you do)

- Send a text once a week to someone and tell them why you think they're awesome (Don't always refer to body parts)

- Let someone into your lane while you're driving. (That's a hard one for me because sometimes some moron gets in front of me and drives 22 miles under the speed limit beside a truck for 18 miles. Oh, sorry. I drive too much.)

- Love your home

- Be patriotic

- Forgive

- *Really* Forgive (moronic drivers and Dick Heads alike)

- Take funeral food, napkins, and toilet paper (to, not from, the bereaved)

- Pick up trash (no reference to people here)

- Teach someone to laugh – do it with them

- Put a quarter in a meter that's about to expire

- Listen – it's a silent skill

- Send a card

- Try to save a drug addict. Find a place they could go for help. Just try…

- Hug your family and friends

- Refrain from cursing or being naked in public (that will make everyone happy)

- Buy a handful of flowers and hand them out. (You'll look daft, but it'll make someone happy)

- Make it your goal to fill someone with confidence

- Make someone laugh (I've found that tripping into a store display tower of Spaghetti-O's works)

- Make someone else's day with a genuine compliment

- Make squirrel soup for your boss; give her the recipe after she compliments it

There is more you can do. If you know of someone in need, you know what to do. Just make sure that families and children in your community have food every day and that the children have a new pair of shoes every year. Leave a beautifully-wrapped treat on someone's front porch with a tag that says: "Have a Wonderful Day – You Deserve It!"

Nothing will ever make you feel any better than helping someone else. I promise you; this is the one absolute truth of life. Do something kind; pay it forward, and enjoy every opportunity to make someone's day better.

Listen to the song "Give a Little Bit." Then take the hand of a lonely person … you'll be surprised how much it enriches both of your lives. Give a little bit of your life to someone.

"We make a living by what we get; we make a life by what we give"
~ Winston Churchill

DOiT Journal:

- How will you make life better for someone else?

- How will you be the reason someone smiles today?

- List things you do for others.

- Think of something new you will do for someone this week to create happiness.

Step 10
Arms Wide Open

"The future is looking back with open arms to welcome you with admiration and delight." ~ Debbie Seagle

You've come a long way baby.

Wherever you are, just look how far you have come. And here you are. You are not the heartsick mortal who shuffled through her misery. You are lively, spirited, and magnificent. You have confidence and charisma. Feel sane again! Take charge of your feelings. Please choose to do so.

You may not have landed exactly where you aimed to go, but you are closer to your destination than you were before you got here. If you didn't follow that, it's okay. Lead the way now. You are where you are meant to be, and you are making the decisions now.

You are the captain of your ship, the author of your story, beginning now. You know the ending; it is astounding! Now, write an incredibly liberating and novel future. Your page is blank. Fill it with your desired purpose and plans to reach your ultimate port.

Whatever your dreams may be, it's up to you to make them come true. Here's How:

- Make a plan
- Set goals (number them)
- Align your goals with your plan and work on your goals (one by one)
- Every day, do more and do better than the day before, and…
- Do everything with purpose

You may notice that everywhere you look, you see a couple kissing, holding hands, laughing together, or picking out cucumbers in the grocery store. Ugly couples, old couples, beautiful couples, topless, and toothless couples... they're everywhere in every alleyway. bookstore, and bait shop.

It's a natural phenomenon to want love again someday ... if not already. Just be prepared to flounder. Before you start scheduling internet dates like a bad series of dead-end job interviews, write Your story first, and be everything you want to be. Once you know who YOU are, it will be easier to know the type of person you want to be with.

On dating sites, you'll find plenty o' men. It's my suspicion that a high percentage of them were recruited from a mental ward. Most of them want to slobber all over your face, move in on you (in every sense of the word), and/or is a "consultant." *Is a consultant some sort of professional expert sage specialist in dating, or what?* You have to wonder. But don't.

Don't let your friend fix you up with a very nice man who has been through a lot. Even if he is "kinda cute" and "takes good care of his cats."

Another friend may offer: "How about my nephew? Ok, he has issues, but doesn't everyone?"

Why not, you love a man who "games professionally" and drinks beer in his mom's basement all day, right?

Beware the friend who wants to introduce you to this tall handsome, wealthy guy in his late 50s who doesn't look a day over 40. He has no baggage; no children; he's never been married.

Yeah, there's a reason for everything.

Don't start fishing to lure whatever takes your bait. Be mindful about the port you choose to dock, if at all.

Early sailors didn't fear losing sight of the shore, they feared that whatever was beyond their vision was a vast nothingness. The ends of the earth. Being alone isn't the end of the world. Cruise. Be patient.

Go with the flow and allow the current to take you somewhere you've never been before. Take a chance on yourself and explore your ideas now that everything isn't about what Dick Head wants, needs, or expects. From You.

Cut the anchors; set sail on the journey of YOU. Chart your own course. Ride the waves. Weather the storms with the skills you've mastered. Don't panic or feel desperate. Your boat will come in when the tide turns your way.

That's essentially all of the seafaring metaphors I could come up with.

Well, one more thing: There are plenty of fish in the sea. But are you really focused on fishing now?

Focus on You. Strive to fulfill your dreams. You may need time alone to figure it out. Rest assured that you don't need a man to make you happy. No man is going to solve your problems. You want a man who won't *become* your problems.

If you meet someone and feel you want more than friendship, be sure you love his qualities, his kindness, his sense of humor, and (you know) – his other stuff. Don't waste your time being his lover (or his friend) if he doesn't make you feel like a happier, better person when you are together.

Rejoice in the fact that you can make your life what you want it to be. The cost of not following your heart, or your dreams, is spending the rest of your life wishing you had.

Discover just how incredible your life can be – because of your very own decisions … the ones you choose and make on your own. Take advantage of this exciting opportunity called Your future.

So, find what you want. It doesn't need to be another person right away.

- It only takes one person to make you happy: You.
- It only takes one person to rule your world: You.
- It only takes one person to finally Get Over Dick Head. (Guess who?)

Here is where your life begins … with your arms wide open, starting with the innocence and hopes of your childhood. Remember how it feels to swing as high as you can – or go down the slide backward. Don't be afraid. Don't overthink the fun out of letting yourself slide.

Feel the delight of mud squishing between your toes. If your childhood wasn't so great, it's never too late to get muddy feet and giggle. Simply put your thumbs in your ears, stick out your tongue, wiggle your fingers, and laugh. Now is a good time for that! DOiT.

Be that little girl sitting on a porch swing with her grandmother or eating a worm to impress the cute little boy down the street. <u>Hint</u>: You don't have to eat worms anymore; there are more alluring ways to hook a guy these days.

That hopeful, optimistic (sometimes stupid) girl is still in you. Call her to come out to play again, and dance in the rain. You are responsible for your own happiness, and you can choose whether to feel miserable or happy. True fact.

Pull out that level of joy and innocence to write the remainder of your fresh new story. What happened yesterday no longer exists. Today is a whole new day, and you are the heroine in your story. Jump in. Float on your back, looking up into the sun, with your arms wide open.

Today is where your book begins, and rewrites are accepted. The future is always unwritten. How exciting that you have your permission to start an entirely new life at this very moment.

Put a restraining order on your negative thoughts and feelings. Actually doing the activities in this book will make you happier. If you don't try laughing yoga, deciding to trust your own dreams, or offering kindness to strangers, how will you know for sure?

DOiT. What do you have to lose?

You are worthy of everything you want from life. You are bold, unstoppable, and fabulous! Enjoy the discoveries, work toward your dreams, and don't let anyone stop you. (Especially not yourself.) You can never fail (unless you stop trying).

Dick Head can't screw with you now. He has been forgiven, released, and joyfully replaced with your selected ambitions. You are so exquisitely independent that you will get over him – if you haven't already.

"Whether you think you can or think you can't, You're Right."
~ Henry Ford

DOiT Journal:

- What is your #1 dream for your future?

- What is your plan for reaching that dream?

- What goals will you set to make your plan succeed?

- What is something amazing about your life at this very moment?

- Five traits you find appealing in another person.

- As you drink your coffee each morning, write down one thing you will do for yourself. DOiT that day. Then add another goal for yourself.

Highlight this. Write it down. Tape it to your mirror:

- This moment in my life is all there is
- I am in my present with peace, hope, love, and joy
- I believe in the infinite possibilities for my future
- I welcome change
- I am in charge of my decisions
- I will follow my dreams with my arms wide open

You are brave, intelligent, and courageous, and you are healing as every moment passes.

You are more loveable than you have ever been before.

You are magnificent!

You are over Dick Head. He doesn't rule your world. Open your heart. Open your arms. Go live a beautiful, happy life – the way *You* want to live it!

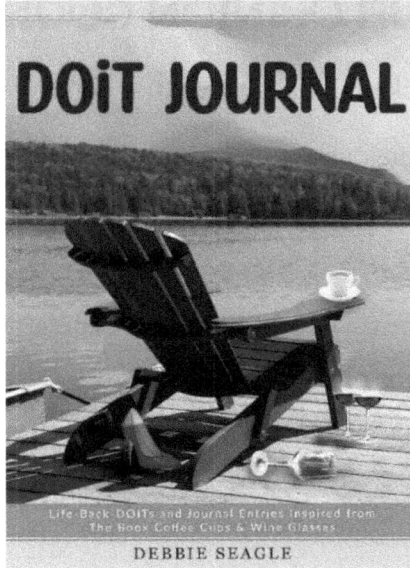

Get Your Free DOiT Journal At
https://www.lifebackdoit.com/

Includes Journal Prompts & DOiTs
Inspired by the book *Coffee Cups & Wine Glasses*

YOUR OPINION COUNTS!

I'd love your feedback and appreciate what you have to say.

Please take two minutes now to leave a review wherever you purchased your book and let me know what you think!

Thank You, Truly,

Debbie

P.S.

Follow me And, your honest review is cherished on:

Amazon

Barnes & Noble

Books A Million

Good Reads

BookBub

PS Your written review could launch your "Influencer" career.

BIOGRAPHY

Debbie Seagle lives in the Blue Ridge Mountains of Virginia where her #1 bestselling book, *Coffee Cups & Wine Glasses*, was written.

She has lived in Hawaii, D.C., New Orleans, Paris, Jordan, Oman, Jacksonville, New Bern, Dublin, and various places in between, but nothing says home like mountain lakes, fresh air, changing seasons, and the incredible people of Southwest Virginia.

Debbie has written Top-Secret technical books, proposals, manuals, and communications. She authored a Sunday column in New Orleans, various newsletters, newspaper articles, magazine features, and U.S. Embassy newspapers.

Other vocations in Debbie Seagle's resume include airshow director, event planner, marketing director, lifeguard, air-to-air photographer, shampoo girl, operations manager, trainer/teacher, military wife, MiMi, and mom extraordinaire.

Family, friends, skiing, sailing, gardening, hiking, kayaking, her truck, good wine, and beautiful wine glasses make her happy.

Despite degrees, certifications, and certificates for various vocations, she still can't juggle.

DOiT Books by Debbie Seagle:

- **Coffee Cups & Wine Glasses**

- **10 Steps to Get Over Dick Head**

- **DOiT Journal https://www.lifebackdoit.com/**

- **DOiT Bullet Journal** (up next with the possibility of a new title)

More books coming soon including a
Children's Christmas Book Series